K M A Ahamed Zubair

Arwi or Arabu-Tamil Handwriting Workbook

K M A Ahamed Zubair

Arwi or Arabu-Tamil Handwriting Workbook

(Arwi - English - Tamil)

Noor Publishing

Imprint
Any brand names and product names mentioned in this book are subject to trademark, brand or patent protection and are trademarks or registered trademarks of their respective holders. The use of brand names, product names, common names, trade names, product descriptions etc. even without a particular marking in this work is in no way to be construed to mean that such names may be regarded as unrestricted in respect of trademark and brand protection legislation and could thus be used by anyone.

Cover image: www.ingimage.com

Publisher:
Noor Publishing
is a trademark of
Dodo Books Indian Ocean Ltd., member of the OmniScriptum S.R.L Publishing group
str. A.Russo 15, of. 61, Chisinau-2068, Republic of Moldova Europe
Printed at: see last page
ISBN: 978-620-4-72241-2

Arwi or Arabu-Tamil

Handwriting Workbook

(Arwi - English - Tamil)

Dr.K.M.A.Ahamed Zubair
Assistant Professor of Arabic,
The New College,
Chennai 600 014, India

الدكتور ك.م.ع. أحمد زب.ير
الأستاذ المساعد، القسم العربي
الكلية الجديدة
تشنائي – 600014، الهند

Editor-in-Chief: NOVA Journal
of Arabic Studies, Canada

مجلة "نوفا" للدراسات **:رئيس التحرير**
العربية (المجلة المحكمة)، كندا

Editor: International Journal
of Literature ,Language and
Linguistics, USA

المجلة الدولية لـ"IJLLL" مجلة **:المحرر**
لأدب واللغة وعلم اللغة (المجلة
المحكمة)، الولايات المتحدة الأمريكية

This Work is dedicated to the
Theologians, Jurists and Philosophers
of India

Contents

Preface

The Arab Muslim traders and the native Tamil converts to Islam in Tamil Nadu state of India, and Sri Lanka came into closer contact as a result of their commercial activities. They were bound by a common religion, but separated by two different languages. They felt the necessity for a link language. They started to write Tamil in an adapted Arabic script called Arwi. From eighth century to nineteenth century, this language enjoyed its popularity among Tamil speaking Muslims of Tamil Nadu and Sri Lanka. The valuable and useful ideas of Tamil Muslim minds were conveyed in Arabicized Tamil called Arwi. It rendered a most useful service for the advancement and progress of Arab and Tamil cultures. However, the beginning of the twentieth century saw the decline of *this* language. And no step was taken to arrest this decline. This book will serve as a guide to master Arwi Script thoroughly with exercises.

1.0 Introduction:

Arwi was used extensively by the Muslims of Tamil Nadu of India and Sri Lanka. This language was devised as a means of communication and interaction of the settled Arabs of Tamil Nadu with the Tamil people. It is a result of the cultural synthesis between seafaring Arabs and the native Tamil-speaking Muslims. It was popular in Tamil Nadu and Ceylon. It has a rich body of literature of which some of them were preserved. There are historical records of the prevalence of Arwi in far Eastern countries, such as Indonesia and Thailand.

Arwi served as a medium of transformation of the Muslim Tamil society of Tamil Nadu and Sri Lanka in their daily affairs to write many religious, literary and poetry texts for communication. The Arwi script represents the Tamil language (having left-to-right script) using an Arabic style of script (having right-to-left script). The Arwi script was widely used by the Muslim Tamils of Asia for their day-to-day communication. From the eighth century to the nineteenth century, this language enjoyed its popularity among Tamil-speaking Muslims of Tamil Nadu and Ceylon. It continues to enjoy the same popularity with the Muslims of Ceylon even today. The Tamil-speaking Muslims of Ceylon consider this Arwi literature as their most beloved literature (Rahim, 415-16).

The similarities of the socio-religious paradigms of the Muslims of South India and Sri Lanka are quite enormous. These may be summarized as follows (Maharoof, 409):

a. The home language of Sri Lankan Muslims and those of Tamil Nadu is Tamil.

b. The Muslim Tamil (spoken at home) in Sri Lanka and Tamil Nadu is a dialect in that it has substantial number of Turko-Perso-Arabic loan words

c. There are close cultural systems between the Muslims of Sri Lanka and Tamil Nadu

d. Muslim Missionaries in Tamil Nadu throughout the ages have entered Sri Lanka and helped shape the religious thinking of the Muslims of Sri Lanka. These Muslim missionaries helped in the establishment of Tariqa. Most of the Qadiriyyah sub-fraternities in Sri Lanka originate from their headquarters in Kilakarai, Kayalpattanam and Kottaru. Kilakarai and

Kayalpattanam are ports in Ramnad and Tirunelveli districts respectively. Kottaru is a town in Tamil Nadu, close to the Kerala state.

2.0 Origin of Arwi:

Arwi was used by the Arabs who came and settled in Tamil Nadu. The settled Arabs in Tamil Nadu learnt Tamil through Arabic Script and wrote Tamil in Arabic script. It is believed that the origin of Arwi is as old as contact of Arabs with Tamil Nadu (Rahman, P. 23). The Muslim communities of Sarandib (Sri Lanka) and **Tamil Nadu** were able to use this language as an effective shield for the preservation of their cultural identity. They were able to safeguard their culture without sacrificing their religion (Shuaib, 91). Arwi was the product of the cultural synthesis between the Arabs and the Tamil speaking Muslims. It is a combination of Arabic and Tamil, but written in Arabic script. After the advent of Islam the Arabs who already settled down in the area naturally became the representatives of Islam in these areas. In course of time, there were also converts to Islam from among the native population. When two communities, bounded by a common religion but separated by two different languages, came into closer contacts, a result of their commercial activities, they felt the necessity for a link-language. This ultimately gave birth to the Arwi language. Arwi represents the fusion of two great languages, belonging to the great ethnic groups, one being the Semitic-Arabic and the other the Dravidian-Tamil.

The Arabs of Tamil Nadu wanted to learn Tamil, which was also an ancient language like Arabic. They started learning Tamil with the help of their own Arabic script. Having learnt this, they started conveying their ideas in this newly originated and newly blended language. In early days, the Arabs were accustomed with colloquial style, when they adopted this they completely ignored Tamil Grammar. They used Tamil Language in daily life as the English men used it in later days. It must be noted that the Arabs before writing the Tamil in Arabic script, used to remember orally most of the words of daily use. Later they put the same in Arabic script. This way the Arwi language was originated in Tamil Nadu (Samuel, 273). In the beginning, the

Arabians conveyed their ideas in words and the Tamilians absorbed, grasped and adopted these words and used them in their daily life and these words were considered to be most important ones for commercial purposes. Even today most of these words are in use. They are used not only by the Tamilians but also by the people of India. Following are the words of Arabic which are in common use (Rahman, 25): Amul (عمل), Asal Aajar (أصل,) حاضر), Kaidi (قيدي), Kajana (خزانة), Mahajar Jamin (مهجر,)(), Dawa (دواء), Jilla Diwan (ديوان,)ضامن Mile ميل (,)نقل Nakal (,)تعلق Taluk (,)جيلا ( ), Jabthi (ضبط), Ameena (أمينة), Masoda (مسودة), Munsif (منصف), Wakkil (وكيل), Inam (إنعام), Sharathu (شرط), Mahsool (محصول), Wasool (وصول), Mirasa (ميراث), Varisu (وارث), Layak (لائق), Baqi (باقي), Jawabu (جواب), Kamm (كم), Sharbath (شربت), Jubba (جبات), Faisal (فيصل), Thakararu (تكرار), Raseedu Pasali(,)رصيد( ), Maamul (معمول), Maidanam فصلي [(Maidan)(ميدان)], Vagaiyera (وغيره)...etc.

Again, Tamil words lack the capacity to convey the full significance of the Islamic terms like Rasul (رسول), Sahabah (صحابه), Wajib (واجب), Jannath (جنة), Jahannam (جهنم), Iman (إيمان), Taqwa (تقوى) etc., (their respective meanings are Messenger, Companions of the Prophet, Obligatory, Paradise, Hell, Belief, Piety...etc). Therefore Arwi words are used in these cases for better expression and understanding. Hence the Tamil Muslims naturally preferred the Arwi Language. The new language was shaped in a manner that retains all the basic aspects of the finest spoken Tamil, and all of its grammatical forms, put on the beautiful garb of the Arabic script. Arabic letters with suitably added diacritical marks were devised. Arwi still has a place among the more traditional Indian Tamil Muslim and Sri Lankan Moor families. Today, it exists only informally in the speech of the Tamil spoken Muslims, as many words unique to it are used in their spoken Tamil. Some of these words that constitute daily conversations among Muslims for example are: Museebah (مصيبة), Mowth (موت), Janazah (جنازة), Raahat (راحة), Shifaa (شفاء), Khair (خير), Wallahi (والله), Ta'lim (تعليم), Kitaab (كتاب), Shaitaan (شيطان), Sharbath (شربت), Sahan (صحن), Baith بيعة Bi'ath (بيت)(), Shirk (شرك), Tayyib (طيب) and Ikhlaas (إخلاص).

3.0 Place of Origin:

The fact that Arwi was prevalent in Colombo, Kayalpattinam, Kilakarai indicates that it was in use, as early as the eighth century of the Christian era (Samuel, 275). The Arabs and the Tamil Muslim might have played their role equally in the formation of Arwi It is the logical result of joint efforts of the Arabs and the Tamil Muslims. It originated in South-West Coast of Ceylon as well as in the South-East Coast of India, more particularly in Kayalpattinam. This language was enriched, promoted and developed in Kayalpattinam. It rendered a most useful service for the advancement and progress of Arab culture and Tamil culture.

4.0 Tamil, Arabic and Arwi Scripts:

Arabic follows a consonantal system.ie it has distinct symbols or letters only for consonants, while the vowels are optional and not represented by separate letters but by a few diacritical marks without which Arabic texts can still be readable and understood. Arabic has 28 consonants and it is written usually from right to left.

Tamil has 30 basic letters comprising 12 vowels 18

consonants and follows essentially a syllabic system of writing, the combination of the consonant and the vowel is represented by a syllabic symbols or letters. Tamil has 216 syllabic symbols or letters apart from the basic symbols or letters of vowels and consonants and it is written from left to right.

The Tamil script

Tamil script of Vowels, Consonants and Syllabic Letters

	அ	ஆ	இ	ஈ	உ	ஊ	எ	ஏ	ஐ	ஒ	ஓ	ஔ
க்	க	கா	கி	கீ	கு	கூ	கெ	கே	கை	கொ	கோ	கௌ
ங்	ங	ஙா	ஙி	ஙீ	ஙு	ஙூ	ஙெ	ஙே	ஙை	ஙொ	ஙோ	ஙௌ
ச்	ச	சா	சி	சீ	சு	சூ	செ	சே	சை	சொ	சோ	சௌ
ஞ்	ஞ	ஞா	ஞி	ஞீ	ஞு	ஞூ	ஞெ	ஞே	ஞை	ஞொ	ஞோ	ஞௌ
ட்	ட	டா	டி	டீ	டு	டூ	டெ	டே	டை	டொ	டோ	டௌ
ண்	ண	ணா	ணி	ணீ	ணு	ணூ	ணெ	ணே	ணை	ணொ	ணோ	ணௌ
த்	த	தா	தி	தீ	து	தூ	தெ	தே	தை	தொ	தோ	தௌ
ந்	ந	நா	நி	நீ	நு	நூ	நெ	நே	நை	நொ	நோ	நௌ
ப்	ப	பா	பி	பீ	பு	பூ	பெ	பே	பை	பொ	போ	பௌ

Tamil script of Vowels, Consonants and Syllabic Letters

ம்	ம	மா	மி	மீ	மு	மூ	மெ	மே	மை	மொ	மோ	மௌ
ய்	ய	யா	யி	யீ	யு	யூ	யெ	யே	யை	யொ	யோ	யௌ
ர்	ர	ரா	ரி	ரீ	ரு	ரூ	ரெ	ரே	ரை	ரொ	ரோ	ரௌ
ல்	ல	லா	லி	லீ	லு	லூ	லெ	லே	லை	லொ	லோ	லௌ
வ்	வ	வா	வி	வீ	வு	வூ	வெ	வே	வை	வொ	வோ	வௌ
ழ்	ழ	ழா	ழி	ழீ	ழு	ழூ	ழெ	ழே	ழை	ழொ	ழோ	ழௌ
ள்	ள	ளா	ளி	ளீ	ளு	ளூ	ளெ	ளே	ளை	ளொ	ளோ	ளௌ
ற்	ற	றா	றி	றீ	று	றூ	றெ	றே	றை	றொ	றோ	றௌ
ன்	ன	னா	னி	னீ	னு	னூ	னெ	னே	னை	னொ	னோ	னௌ
ஃ												

Arabic Script

خ	ح	ج	ث	ت	ب	أ
kha'	h'aa'	jiim	thaa'	taa'	baa'	alif
ص	ش	س	ز	ر	ذ	د
saad	shiin	siin	zaay	raa'	thaal	daal
ق	ف	غ	ع	ظ	ط	ض
qaaf	feh'	ghayn	'ayn	thaa	Taa'	daad
ي	و	ه	ن	م	ل	ك
yaa'	waaw	haa	nuun	miim	laam	kaaf

The Arwi script represents the Tamil language using an Arabic style of scripts. In addition to Arabic script, 12 characters were added. It is conveniently written with vowels. For those vowels which also exist in Arabic, that is -a-, -i-, -u-, -aa-, -ii-, -uu-, and the diphthongs -ai- and -au-, the same signs are in use that are used in Arabic, i.e. *fatha*, *qasra* and *damma* for the short vowels , long vowel being indicated by additional *alif*, *yaa* and *waaw*, respectively, and the diphthongs being written with *fatha* (-a-) plus *yaa* or *waaw*. In addition to the basic Arabic letters, several characters have been introduced to write

Tamil sounds not found in Arabic.

The Arwi consists of 40 letters, out of which 28 letters are from Arabic and 12 letters are devised by adding some marks and dots to the original Arabic Alphabet. Eighteen Arabic letters do not have their equivalents in Tamil from the phonetic point of view and similarly ten Tamil letters and two vowel sounds have no equivalents in Arabic. Thus the Arwi alphabet is the Arabic alphabet with the devised twelve additional letters to represent the Tamil vowels and several Tamil consonants that could not be mapped to Arabic sounds.

Arwi Script (in Fonts)

ت ث ج چ ح خ د ڊ د ذ ي ذ ر ڔ ز س ش ص ۚ ص ض ا ب
ۻ ن م ل ك ڮ ق ڣ ف غ ع ظ ط ض ن ي وه-

Arwi Script

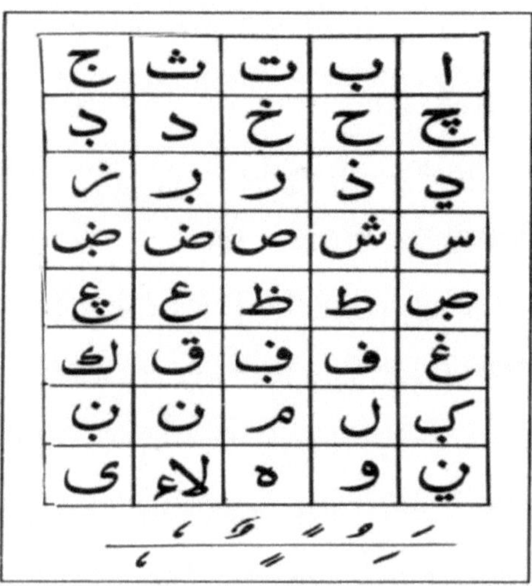

There are eighteen Arabic letters which do not have their equivalents in Tamil from the phonetic point of view. There are seven Arwi letters which have their equivalents in English language.

ش	ز	ذ	د	خ	ح	ج	ث	ب
ه	ق	ف	غ	ع	ظ	ط	ض	ص

5.0 Arwi letters, Its Equivalent Tamil Letters and Phonetic Sound Equivalents in English - A Glance:

ذ	د	خ	ح	چ	ج	ث	ت	ب	ا
ட்	த்	க்க்	ஹ்ற	ச்ச்	ஜ், ச்	ஸ்	த்த்	ப்	
ṭ	t	kk	h	cc	j, c	s	tt	p	'/-
[ṭ]	[t:]	[k:]	[h]	[tʃ:]	[dʒ/tʃ]	[s]	[t:]	[p]	[ʔ]
ض	صٜ	ص	ش	س	ز	رٜ	ر	ذ	ذ
த்	ள்	ஸ்	ஷ், ஶ்	ஸ்	ஂஜ்	ர்	ற்	ஂஜ்	ட்ட்
t	l	s	ṣ, ś	s	z	r	ɽ	z	ṭṭ
[t]	[ll]	[s]	[ṣ/ʃ]	[s]	[z]	[ɽ]	[r]	[z/s]	[t:]
ك	ق	ف	ف	غ	▢	ع	ظ	ط	ض
க்க்	க்க்	ப்	ஂப்	க்	ங		ஂஜ்	த்த்	ழ்
kk	kk	p	f	k	ṅ	'	z	tt	ḻ
[k:]	[k:]	[p]	[f/p]	[k]	[ŋ]	[ʔ]	[z/s]	[t:]	[ɻ]
	ي	و	ه	ن	ن	ن	م	ل	▢
	ய்	வ்	ஹ்ற	ஞ்	ண்	ந்,ன்	ம்	ல்	க்
	y	w	h	ñ	ṇ	n, ṉ	m	l	k
	[j]	[ʋ]	[h]	[ɲ]	[ɳ]	[ṉ/n]	[m]	[l]	[k]
					'	'	`	▢	ٗ
					உ	ஓ	இ	எ	அ
					u	o	i	e	a
					[u]	[o]	[i]	[e]	[a]
			وَ	يَ	وُ	وُ	يِ	▢ي	ٱ ,ٮ
			ஔ	ஐ	ஊ	ஓ	FF	ஏ	ஆ
			au	ai	ū	ō	ī	ē	ā

		[aɻ]	[aɪ]	[uː]	[oː]	[iː]	[eː]	[aː]

The 11 Tamil letters and two vowels sounds which have no equivalent in Arabic are:
ச, ச, ட, ட (as in படம்), ட (as in பட்டம்), ள, ட,ற (as a different from ற) ப, க (as in சங்கம்) and the two vowels are எ & ஒ

Tamil	Arwi	English	Pronunciation
ச்ச	چ	Cha	Cha in Chance
ட	دْ	Da	Da in Dawn
்ட	دِ	Ta	Ta in Top
ற	ر	Ra	R (soft ر)
ழ	ض	Zha	Unique in Arwi
ப	ڢ	Pa	Pa in Pause
ண	ن	Na	Unique in Arwi
ஞ	نْ	Gna	Unique in Arwi
ஒ	◌ْ	O	O in Pot
ள	صْ	La	Strong L
ங	ع	Nga	Ng in Bang
க	ك	Ga	Go in Gold
எ	۔	E	E in Men

6.0 Formation and Construction of Eleven Arwi letters and Two vowel marks from the existing Arabic Alphabet (Zubair,2014,60-62):

1. To the already existing dot ح , two more dots are added to make the Tamil ச thus چ (pronounced as the 'ch' in much).

2. Below the letter د is added a dot, to make it the equivalent of Tamil ட (as in பாடம்) thus ڊ (pronounced a as the 'd' in 'Burden').

3. By placing two dots under د , the sound of ட (as in பட்டம்) may be obtained, which is equivalent to 'T' in English. It is written as ڌ

4. While for the Tamil ற the Arabic is used in its original form, for the Tamil ர, a dot is put under the same Arabic letter thus ڔ , which is 'R' in English.

5. A dot added below ض gives the sound of ழ, in Tamil (as in பழம்). It is obtained thus ظ This letter has no equivalent in English but the two English letters, 'zh' convey the sound when written together.

6. By placing a dot below ص the Tamil sound ள is obtained, (as in பள்ளம்) This letter is writen as ڝ and it also has no equivalent in English.

7. By adding three dots under the Arabic letter ع the Tamil letter ங is produced thus ڠ (pronounced as the 'ng' in 'Going').

8. By adding a dot below ف the soft Tamil ப (as in பசி) is obtained thus ڣ equivalent of P (This shows that Arwi was never influenced by Persian at all in its evolution because, the 'p' in Persian language is made by adding two more dots to ب thus پ

9. The sound of 'G' (as in சங்கம்) has been obtained by placing a dot below ك resulting in ڬ which is 'G' as in 'God'.

10. The sound of the Tamil letter ண (which has no English equivalent) is obtained by adding below ن dot thus ڹ

11. By adfing two dots below the letter ن in the Arabic alphabet, we Get ஞ (as in தஞ்சம்). This letter is written thus ݧ and it also has no equivalent in English but the sound may be indicated by using the English letters 'g' and 'n' together as 'gn' (as in 'sign').

12. For producing the vowel sound of ஒ (pronounced as the 'o' in 'wonder'), the sign ٗ is put on top of any letter. This is called Ko Pesh).

13. By putting the same sign ٖ under a letter, the vowel sound of எ (pronounced as the e in Men) is produced. This is called Ko Zayr

Arwi letters arranged according to the Arabic Alphabetical order

ض	صٜ	ص	ش	س	ز	ر	ر	ذ	دٜ	دِ	د	خ	ح	چ	ج	ث	ت	ب	ا
	ள		ஷ	ஸ	ஃஜ	ற	ர		ண்ட	ட	த	ஃக		ச்ச	ஜ		த		அ
ḍ	l	ṣ	sh	s	z	r	ṛ	dh	T	D	d	kh	ḥ	ch	j	th	t	b	a

ي	و	ه	نٜ	ن	ن	م	ل	كٜ	ك	ق	ب	ف	غ	ع	ع	ظ	ط	ض
ய	வ	ஹ	ஞ	ண	ன	ம	ல	க	க்க		ப	ஃப		ங				ழ
y	w	h	ñ	ṇ	n	m	l	g	k	q	p	f	gh	ng	'	ẓ	ṭ	zh

There are seven Arwi letters, which have their equivalents in English Language. These letters are:

م	mīm	M	As in English
ن	nūn	N	As in English
و	wāw	W	As in English
ه	hey	H	As in English
لا	lām alif	LA	As in English
ي	ya or yey	Y	As in English
ء	hamzah	A	As in English

7.0 Specimen of Arwi writing (Hand written) (Zubair, 2014, 65-66):

(Transliteration of the above Invitation in Tamil)

சோனக இஸ்லாமிய கலாச்சார நிலையம் (அமைக்கப்பட்டது)

தங்களுக்கு எமது நல்வாழ்த்தும் சோபனமும் கூறுவதோடு கொழும்பு கோட்டை பிரிஸ்டல் வீதி, 27 ஆம் நம்பர் இல்லமாகிய இஸ்லாமிய கலாச்சார நிலைய புதுக்கட்டிட திறப்பு விழாவிற்கு 1965, மே மாதம் 30 ஆம் தேதி, ஹிஜ்ரா 1385 முஹர்ரம் 28 பிறை ஞாயிறு பிற்பகல் 4:15 மணிக்கு சங்கமிக்குமாறு தங்களை அன்புடன் அழைக்கிறோம்.

கௌரவ பிரதமர் திரு.டட்லி சோனானாயக அவர்கள் ஞாபகார்த்த பலகையை திரை நீக்கம் செய்வார்கள். தலைமை நிலையத் தலைவர் ஜனாப் சர் ராஜிக் ஃபரீத் அவர்கள் புதுக்கட்டிடத்தை திறந்து வைப்பார்கள்.

(Translation of the above Invitation in English)

Sonaga[1] Islamic Cultural Centre (Established)

We send you our felicitations, greetings and cordially invite you to attend the opening ceremony of our new building at No. 27 Bristol Street, Fort, Colombo, on the 30th May, 1965, the 28th Day of Muharram 1385, Sunday afternoon, 4:15 pm.

Honourable Prime Minister Mr. Dudley Senanayake will unveil the commemoration block. The President of the centre, Sir Razik Fareed will open the building.

8.0 Specimen of Arwi writing (Computer encoded):

The following are the few couplets of an Arwi poem written by Syed Mohammed Imam al-Aroos (1816-1898 A.D):

يِنّيَا ضُمْ وَلُّوۡڹ يِيۡبَكَانْتَ نَاثَا

تَنّيَرِيۡمْ تَـوَنّْ تَنْتَا ضَكُوَايِنِ

(Transliteration of the above couplet in Tamil)

என்னை ஆளும் வல்லோனே ஏகாந்த நாதா

தன்னை அறியும் தவத்தை தந்தாள்குவாய் நீ

(Translation of the above couplet in English)

O Almighty Who rules over me! O my Master who is the only Lord!

Bless me with the boon of realizing the insignificance of myself.

اُنَّيَّلَّاثُ وِيُرْيَارَىْ وِضْفِّيْنْ

يِنَّىْ وِجُّمْحَقَّاكَ اُتِّلْ اَضِفِّيْنْ

(Transliteration of the above couplet in Tamil)

உன்னை அல்லாது வேறு யாரை விளிப்பேன்
என்னை விட்டும் ஹக்காக உன்னில் ஒளிப்பேன்

(Translation of the above couplet in English)

Whom can I beseech except Thee!

I will [leave my wretched self and] annihilate in Thee!

)

The following is the table of four Tamil letters and their Arwi equivalents

Tamil Letter	Arwi Letter	Tamil Letter	Arwi Letter	Tamil Letter	Arwi Letter	Tamil Letter	Arwi Letter
த்	تْ	ந்	نْ	ம்	مْ	ல்	لْ
த	تَ	ந	نَ	ம	مَ	ல	لَ
தா	تَا	நா	نَا	மா	مَا	லா	لَا
தி	تِ	நி	نِ	மி	مِ	லி	لِ
தீ	تِيْ	நீ	نِيْ	மீ	مِيْ	லீ	لِيْ
து	تُ	நு	نُ	மு	مُ	லு	لُ
தூ	تُوْ	நூ	نُوْ	மூ	مُوْ	லூ	لُوْ
தெ	تᷱ	நெ	نᷱ	மெ	مᷱ	லெ	لᷱ
தே	تᷕي	நே	نᷕي	மே	مᷕي	லே	لᷕي
தை	تَيْ	நை	نَيْ	மை	مَيْ	லை	لَيْ
தொ	تُ	நொ	نُ	மொ	مُ	லொ	لُ

9.0 Issues in Encoding Arwi Language with Special Reference to Unicode: A Computational Perspective

Unicode is an industry standard character set encoding developed and maintained by the Unicode Consortium. The Unicode character set is able to support over one million characters, and is being developed with an aim to have a single character set that supports all characters from all scripts, as well as many symbols, that are in common use around the world. Currently, it supports over 94,000 characters representing a large number of scripts. The benefits of a single, universal character set and the practical considerations for implementation that have gone into the design of Unicode have made it a success, and it is well on the way to becoming a dominant one.

For users working with multilingual data, products were often tied to a single encoding; this did not allow users to work with multilingual data or with data coming from incompatible systems. Developers were also required to support multiple versions of their products to serve different markets, making development and deployment for multiple markets a difficult process. In order to support data created using others' products, developers had to support a variety of different standards for a single language. In order to work with multilingual data, they needed to support several standards simultaneously since no one standard supported more than a handful of languages. In turn, it was impossible to support multilingual data in plain text. Developing software that had anything to do with multilingual text have become incredibly difficult.

There were four key original design goals for Unicode:

1. To create a universal standard that covered all writing systems.
2. To use an efficient encoding that avoided mechanisms such as code page switching, shift-sequences and special states.
3. To use a uniform encoding width in which each character was encoded as a 16-bit value.
4. To create an unambiguous encoding in which any given 16-bit value always represented the same character regardless of where it occurred in the

data.

With the rapid integration of Unicode into various software products, the Unicode caters the entire operating systems. All of the characters that you need in Arwi language should be available in Unicode. Unicode effectively puts all characters on the same playing field or level; specifically all characters are given equal treatment. Unicode is an evolving character set which typically means that more and more characters are being added in general and four symbols(three letters and one vowel mark) of Arwi language in particular to its row rather repertoire. Unicode has wide support by various operating systems, software and browsers and thus there is no need to install any new fonts. Instead of developing a font for this Arwi language, we can use the existing Unicode characters from the Semitic group of languages, in order to type in Arwi language. From the Unicode characters present from U+0600 to U+06FF in the range of Arabic and an another character U+0767 available in the range of Syriac language, we can type or encode the entire Arwi language.

The Arwi script faces the encoding problems while typing this Arwi character on computer. And this issue directly affects the printing of Arwi language books. Thus even the printing system demands such common encoding solutions to Arwi language in general, and Unicode characters in particular. So now we analyze the issues pertaining to encode the Arwi scripts in the forthcoming pages.

The Arabic Unicode characters utilized for Arwi script are as follows:

ا	0627		ص	0635		و	0648
ب	0628		ض	0636		ى	0649
ت	062A		ط	0637			
ث	062B		ظ	0638			
ج	062C		ع	0639			
ح	062D		غ	063A			
خ	062E		ف	0641			
د	062F		ق	0642			
ذ	0630		ك	0643			
ر	0631		ل	0644			
ز	0632		م	0645			
س	0633		ن	0646			
ش	0634		ه	0647			

The nine Arwi letters which have no equivalents in Arabic and their Unicode numbers. For four Arwi letters, Unicode characters are not available.

Hence the following Unicode Substitutional characters for the four non-available characters in Arwi script are suggested by me as follows:

Suggested Arwi Character	Tamil Equivalent Character	Specification of the Substitutional Unicode Characters
ڝ	ள	**-Arabic letter *Saad* with two dots below (U+069D)**
ڠ	ங	**-Arabic letter *Ayn* with three dots above (U+06A0)**
ڬ	க	**- Arabic letter *kaaf* with dot above (U+06AC)**
۪	எ	**- Arabic *Empty Centre Low Stop* (U+06EA)**

Thus the Arwi script encoded in Unicode should be as follows:

No.	Arwi Alphabet	Writing / Encoding Remarks
1.	ا	An Arabic Alphabet. Available in Unicode.
2.	ب	An Arabic Alphabet. Available in Unicode.
3.	ت	An Arabic Alphabet. Available in Unicode.
4.	ث	An Arabic Alphabet. Available in Unicode.
5.	ج	An Arabic Alphabet. Available in Unicode.
6.	چ	An Arwi Alphabet .Available in Unicode. Used in Persian and Urdu languages also.
7.	ح	An Arabic Alphabet. Available in Unicode.
8.	خ	An Arabic Alphabet. Available in Unicode.
9.	د	An Arabic Alphabet. Available in Unicode.
10.	ڊ	An Arwi Alphabet. Available in Unicode. Used in Sindhi and Early Persian languages also.
11.	ڍ	An Arwi Alphabet. Available in Unicode. Used in Sindhi language also.

12.	ذ	An Arabic Alphabet. Available in Unicode.
13.	ر	An Arabic Alphabet. Available in Unicode.
14.	ڔ	An Arwi Alphabet. Available in Unicode. Used in Sindhi and Early Persian languages also.
15.	ڹ	An Arabic Alphabet. Available in Unicode.
16.	س	An Arabic Alphabet. Available in Unicode.
17.	ش	An Arabic Alphabet. Available in Unicode.
18.	ص	An Arabic Alphabet. Available in Unicode.
19.	ض	An Arabic Alphabet. Available in Unicode.
20.	ضٜ	An Arwi Alphabet. Available in Unicode. It is an Extended Arabic letter.
21.	ڝ	An Arwi Alphabet. Available in Unicode. Instead of the Arabic letter *Saad* with one dot below, we can employ the Arabic letter *Saad* with two dots below.Used in Turkish language also.

22.	ط	An Arabic Alphabet. Available in Unicode.
23.	ظ	An Arabic Alphabet. Available in Unicode.
24.	ع	An Arabic Alphabet. Available in Unicode.
25.	غ	An Arwi Alphabet. Available in Unicode. Instead of the Arabic letter *Ayn* with three dots below, we can employ the Arabic letter *Ayn* with three dots above. Used in old Malay language also.
26.	غ	An Arabic Alphabet. Available in Unicode.
27.	ف	An Arabic Alphabet. Available in Unicode.
28.	ڧ	An Arwi Alphabet. Available in Unicode. Used in Ingush language spoken in Ingushetia and Uzbekistan
29.	ق	An Arabic Alphabet. Available in Unicode.
30.	ك	An Arabic Alphabet. Available in Unicode.
31.	ڬ	An Arwi Alphabet. Available in Unicode. Instead of the Arabic letter *Kaaf* with one dot below, we can employ the Arabic letter *Kaaf* with one dot above. Used in old Malay language also.

32.	ل	An Arabic Alphabet. Available in Unicode.
33.	م	An Arabic Alphabet. Available in Unicode.
34.	ن	An Arabic Alphabet. Available in Unicode.
35.	ݧ	An Arwi Alphabet. Available in Unicode. Extended Arabic letter also.
36.	ݧ	An Arwi Alphabet. Available in Unicode. Developed exclusively for Arwi language.
37.	و	An Arabic Alphabet. Available in Unicode.
38.	ۀ	An Arabic Alphabet. Available in Unicode.
39.	ى	An Arabic Alphabet. Available in Unicode.
40.	٥	ா/ An Arwi Vowel. Available in Unicode. Instead of the Vowel sign (the symbol like of Apostrophe) placed below the Consonant, we can employ an Arabic *Empty Centre Low Stop* symbol. Used as a Quranic Annotation Sign also.
41.	٬	ூ/ An Arwi Vowel. Available in Unicode. It is a Symbol of Arabic inverted *Dammah* called *Ko Pesh* or *Ulta Pesh.*Used in Kashmiri and Urdu

		Languages also.

16.0 Arwi Keyboard for Mobile Android Users:

This keyboard is developed by my Post Graduate student Mr.Anees Ahmed of Kayalapattinam, pursuing M.A Arabic in the New College, Chennai under my suggestion with due consultation from me.

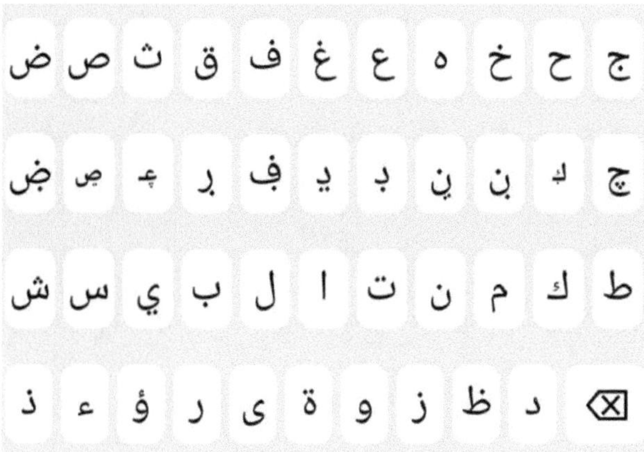

Updated Android Version

ض ص ث ق ف غ ع ه خ ح ج

ض ص ف چ ر پ ک د ي ن ب

ش س ي ب ل ا ت ن م ك ط

ذ ء ؤ ر ى ة و ز ظ د ⌫

۱۲۳ ، اردو . ↵

۰ ۹ ۸ ۷ ۶ ۵ ۴ ۳ ۲ ۱

10.0 Decline of Arwi Language:

Arwi language originated in 8th century, flourished during the medieval ages and saw its decline from the beginning of the twentieth century. In the Globalizational Era, no step was taken to arrest this decline of this language which had the south Asia based cultural and historical background. Today Arwi is known to be a matter of least scholarly interest in some parts of Tamil Nadu state of India and Sri Lanka. This literature did not receive much attention in the later part of the 20th century. Other languages such as English replaced it in many contexts. One most important reason for its decline is the lack of competitive printing facilities. Printing of Arwi books is a very complicated and tedious process. Therefore, people preferred printing their religious books in Tamil rather than in Arwi language. During the early 20th century the adoption of Urdu as the dominant Islamic school curriculum, which is ethnocentrically unconcerned with Arwi which has a different South Asia based cultural and historical background, is also an another reason for its decline.

11.0 Remarks:

In the system of modern education, Muslim children failed to learn Arwi language, as it was out of the school curriculum. In the system of religious educational institutions, the north Indian syllabus known as *Silsilatun Nizamiyyah* was adopted by the *Madrasahs* in the beginning of the twentieth century in Tamil Nadu. Arwi as a language and subject did not find a place in that syllabus.

The decline of Arwi language is a great loss to the Tamil Muslim community as this was their religious language. It had safeguarded the interest of this community. It was fondly and reverently nurtured by noble savants. Therefore, its necessity must be felt by the present Tamil Muslim community. Its revival and renaissance is badly needed. The following steps are suggested to arrest its decline and revitalize its literature for the cultural benefit of particularly the Tamil Muslim Community:

a. All the Arwi language books available should be collected and re-printed. Unpublished manuscripts also should be collected and printed.

b. Arwi language should be made compulsory in all the *Madrasahs* of Tamil Nadu and Sri Lanka.

c. Arwi books must be taught to children attending schools as a part of school curriculum.

d. Arwi community must be encouraged to use it in their daily affairs.

e. Periodicals and magazines in this language should be re-introduced.

With these measures taken we may witness the period of renaissance in Arwi language and literature in the years to come.

Arwi Alphabet

No.	Arwi Alphabet	No.		No.		No.	
1.	ا	11.	ﺑ	22.	ط	33.	م
2.	ب	12.	ذ	23.	ظ	34.	ن
3.	ت	13.	ر	24.	ع	35.	ن
4.	ث	14.	ڔ	25.	چ	36.	ﯨ
5.	ج	15.	ز	26.	غ	37.	و
6.	چ	16.	س	27.	ف	38.	ه
7.	ح	17.	ش	28.	ف	39.	ي
8.	خ	18.	ص	29.	ق	40.	○
9.	د	19.	ﺻ	30.	ك	41.	ء
10.	ﮄ	20.	ض	31.	ك		
		21.	ض	32.	ل		

Letters used in Arwi or Arabu-Tamil

ஃ	அ	ஆ	இ	ஈ	உ	ஊ	எ	ஏ	ஐ	ஒ	ஓ
ஔ											

	a	ā	i	ī	u	ū	e	ē	ai	o	ō	au

க்	k	க	கா	கி	கீ	கு	கூ	கெ	கே	கை	கொ
கோ	கௌ										

ங்	ṅ	ங	ஙா	ஙி	ஙீ	ஙு	ஙூ	ஙெ	ஙே	ஙை	ஙொ
ஙோ	ஙௌ										

ச்	c	ச	சா	சி	சீ	சு	சூ	செ	சே	சை	சொ
சோ	சௌ										

ஞ்	ñ	ஞ	ஞா	ஞி	ஞீ	ஞு	ஞூ	ஞெ	ஞே	ஞை
ஞொ	ஞோ	ஞௌ								

ட்	ṭ	ட	டா	டி	டீ	டு	டூ	டெ	டே	டை	டொ
டோ	டௌ										

ண்	ṇ	ண	ணா	ணி	ணீ	ணு	ணூ	ணெ	ணே
ணை	ணொ	ணோ	ணௌ						

த்	t	த	தா	தி	தீ	து	தூ	தெ	தே	தை	தொ
தோ	தௌ										

ந்	n	ந	நா	நி	நீ	நு	நூ	நெ	நே	நை	நொ
நோ	நௌ										

ப்	p	ப	பா	பி	பீ	பு	பூ	பெ	பே	பை	பொ

போ பெள

ம் ɱ ம மா மி மீ மு மூ மெ மே மைமொ
மோமௌ

ய் y ய யா யி யீ யு யூ யெ யே யையொ
யோ யௌ

ர் r ர ரா ரி ரீ ரு ரூ ரெ ரே ரைரொ
ரோ ரௌ

ல் l ல லா லி லீ லு லூ லெ லே லைலொ
லோ லௌ

வ் v வ வா வி வீ வு வூ வெ வே வைவொ
வோ வௌ

ழ் ḻ ழ ழா ழி ழீ ழு ழூ ழெ ழே ழைழொ
ழோழௌ

ள் ḷ ள ளா ளி ளீ ளு ளூ ளெ ளே ளைளொ
ளோ ளௌ

ற் ṟ ற றா றி றீ று றூ றெ றே றைறொ
றோறௌ

ன் ṉ ன னா னி னீ னு னூ னெனே னை
னொ னோ னௌ

The combining procedures of Arwi are of same as Arabic:

ا ا

ا ا ا ا

ب ب ب ببب

ت ت ت تتت

ث ث ث ثثث

ج جـ جـ جـ جـ ج

حـ حـ حـ د د د

خخ خـ خـ خـ خـ

دد

ذذ

ذ ذ ذ

رر

ر ر ر

زز

ز ز ز

سـ سـ س سس

ش شـ ش ششش

صـ صـ ص صصص

ضـ ضـ ض ضضض

ط ط ط ططط

ظ ظ ظ ظظظ

ط ط ط

ع ع ع ععع

ع ع ع

غ غ غ غغغ

غ غ غ

ف ف ف ففف

ف ف ف

ق ـقـ ق ققق

ككك ك ـكـ ك

للل ل ـلـ ل

ممم م ـمـ م

ﻧ ﺬ ﻥ ﻧﻦ

ﻫ ﻬ ﻪ ﻫﻪ

ﻭﻭ

ﻱ ﻳ ﻲ ﻳﻲ

ث	ت	ب	ا

د	خ	ح	ج

س	ز	ر	ذ

ط	ض	ص	ش

ف	غ	ع	ظ

م	ل	ك	ق

ي	و	ه	ن
ي	و	ه	ن
ي	و	ه	ن
ي	و	ه	ن
ي	و	ه	ن
ي	و	ه	ن

7. Trace	6.write	5.Trace	4.trace	3. Write	2. Trace	1. Trace

7. Trace	6.write	5.Trace	4.trace	3. Write	2. Trace	1. Trace

5.Trace	4.Write	3.Trace	2.Trace / Write		1.Trace	
	2	2	2		2	
	2	2	2		2	

7. Trace	6.write	5.Trace	4.trace	3. Write	2. Trace	1. Trace
ل		ل	ل		ل	ل
م		م	م		م	م
ن		ن	ن		ن	ن
و		و	و		و	و

أَعُوذُ بِاللهِ   السَّمِيعُ الْعَلِيمُ

سُبْحَانَ اللَّهَ   الْغَفُورُ الرَّحِيمُ

وَالْحَمْدُ لِلَّهِ رَبِّ الْعَالَمِينَ

Mastering Arwi Script:

Handwriting Worksheets

அ	ஆ	இ	ஈ	உ	ஊ
a	ā	i	ī	u	ū
أَ	ا	اِ	اِيْ	أُ	أُوْ

எ	ஏ	ஐ	ஒ	ஓ	ஔ
e	ē	ai	o	ō	au
اِ	اِي	اَيْ	اُ	اَوْ	اَوْ

க	கா	கி	கீ	கு	கூ
كَ	گَا	كِ	كِيْ	كُ	كُوْ
Ka	Kaa	Ki	Kii	Ku	Kuu
كَ	گَا	كِ	كِيْ	كُ	كُوْ

கெ	கே	கை	கொ	கோ	கௌ
كِ	كِي	كَيْ	كُ	كُوْ	كَوْ
Ke	Kee	Kai	Ko	Koo	kau

ങ	ങാ	ങി	ങീ	ങു	ങൂ
عَ	عَا	عِ	عِي	عُ	عُوْ
Nga	Ngaa	Ngi	Ngii	Ngu	Nguu

ஙெ	ஙே	ஙை	ஙொ	ஙோ	ஙௌ
عِ	عِي	عَيْ	عُ	عُوْ	عَوْ
Nge	Ngee	Ngai	Ngo	Ngoo	Ngau
ஙெ	ஙே	ஙை	ஙொ	ஙோ	ஙௌ
عِ	عِي	عَيْ	عُ	عُوْ	عَوْ
Nge	Ngee	Ngai	Ngo	Ngoo	Ngau

स	सा	सी	सी	सु	सू
چَ	چَا	چِ	چِي	چُ	چُو
Sa	Saa	Si	Sii	Su	Suu
چَ	چَا	چِ	چِي	چُ	چُو

செ	சே	சை	சொ	சோ	செள
چَ	چِيْ	چَيْ	چَّ	چُوْ	چَوْ
Se	See	Sai	So	Soo	Sau
செ	சே	சை	சொ	சோ	செள

ஞ	ஞா	ஞி	ஞீ	ஞு	ஞூ
نَ	يَا	نِ	نِيْ	نُ	يُوْ
Nja	Njaa	Nji	Njii	Nju	Njuu

நெ	நே	நை	நொ	நோ	நௌ
نِ	نِيْ	نَيْ	نْ	نِوْ	نَوْ
Nje	Njee	Njai	Njo	Njoo	Sjau
نِ	نِيْ	نَيْ	نْ	نِوْ	نَوْ

ᜎ	ᜎᜒᜆ	ᜎᜒ	ᜎᜒ	ᜎᜓ	ᜎᜓ
دَ	دَا	دِ	دِي	دُ	دُوْ
Ta	Taa	Ti	Tii	Tu	Tuu
دَ	دَا	دِ	دِي	دُ	دُوْ

டெ	டே	டை	டொ	டோ	டௌ
دِ	دَيْ	دَيْ	دْ	دَوْ	دَوْ
Te	Tee	Tai	To	Too	tau
டெ	டே	டை	டொ	டோ	டௌ
دِ	دَيْ	دَيْ	دْ	دَوْ	دَوْ
Te	Tee	Tai	To	Too	tau

ண	ணா	ணி	ணீ	ணு	ணூ
نَ	نَا	نِ	نِيْ	نُ	نُوْ
Na	Naa	Ni	Nii	Nu	Nuu
نَ	نَا	نِ	نِيْ	نُ	نُوْ

ணெ	ணே	ணை	ணொ	ணோ	ணௌ
نِ	نٖيْ	نَيْ	نُ	نُو	نَوْ
Ne	Nee	Nai	No	Noo	Nau

த	தா	தி	தீ	து	தூ
تَ	تَا	تِ	تِــيْ	تُ	تُوْ
Tha	Thaa	Thi	Thii	Thu	Thuu
தَ	تَا	تِ	تِــيْ	تُ	تُوْ

தெ	தே	தை	தொ	தோ	தௌ
تِ	تِي	تَيْ	تَ	تُوْ	تَوْ
The	Thee	Thai	Tho	Thoo	Thau
தெ	தே	தை	தொ	தோ	தௌ
تِ	تِي	تَيْ	تَ	تُوْ	تَوْ

ந	நா	நி	நீ	நு	நூ
نَ	نَا	نِ	نِيْ	نُ	نُوْ
na	naa	ni	nii	nu	nuu
نَ	نَا	نِ	نِيْ	نُ	نُوْ
na	naa	ni	nii	nu	nuu

நெ	நே	நை	நொ	நோ	நௌ
نِ	نِيْ	نَيْ	نً	نَوْ	نَوْ
ne	nee	nai	no	noo	nau
نِ	نِيْ	نَيْ	نً	نَوْ	نَوْ

ப	பா	பி	பீ	பு	பூ
فَ	فَا	فِ	فِيْ	فُ	فُوْ
Pa	Paa	Pi	Pii	Pu	Puu

பெ	பே	பை	பொ	போ	பௌ
فِ	فِي	فَي	ف�763	فُو	فَوْ
Pe	Pee	Pai	Po	Poo	Pau

ம	மா	மி	மீ	மு	மூ
مَ	مَا	مِ	مِيْ	مُ	مُوْ
Ma	Maa	Mi	Mii	Mu	Muu

மெ	மே	மை	மொ	மோ	மௌ
مِ	مِي	مَيْ	مُ	مَوْ	مَوْ
Me	Mee	Mai	Mo	Moo	Mau
மெ	மே	மை	மொ	மோ	மௌ
مِ	مِي	مَيْ	مُ	مَوْ	مَوْ

ய	யா	யி	யீ	யு	யூ
يَ	يَا	يِ	يِيْ	يُ	يُوْ
Ya	Yaa	Yi	Yii	Yu	Yuu

யெ	யே	யை	யொ	யோ	யௌ
یِ	پيْ	يَيْ	يُ	يَوْ	يَوْ
Ye	Yee	Yai	Yo	Yoo	yau
யெ	யே	யை	யொ	யோ	யௌ
یِ	پيْ	يَيْ	يُ	يَوْ	يَوْ
Ye	Yee	Yai	Yo	Yoo	yau

ர	ரா	ரி	ரீ	ரு	ரூ
رَ	رَا	رِ	رِي	رُ	رُو
Ra	Raa	Ri	Rii	Ru	Ruu
رَ	رَا	رِ	رِي	رُ	رُو

ரெ	ரே	ரை	ரொ	ரோ	ரௌ
رِ	رِي	رَيْ	رُ	رُوْ	رَوْ
Re	Ree	Rai	Ro	Roo	rau

ல	லா	லி	லீ	லு	லூ
لَ	لَا	لِ	لِيْ	لُ	لُوْ
La	Laa	Li	Lii	Lu	Luu
لَ	لَا	لِ	لِيْ	لُ	لُوْ

ெல	ேல	ைல	ெலா	ேலா	ெளள
لِ	لِيْ	لَيْ	لَ	لُوْ	لَوْ
Le	Lee	Lai	Lo	Loo	lau
ெல	ேல	ைல	ெலா	ேலா	ெளள
لِ	لِيْ	لَيْ	لَ	لُوْ	لَوْ

வ	வா	வி	வீ	வு	வூ
وَ	وَا	وِ	وِيْ	وُ	وُوْ
Va	Vaa	Vi	Vii	Vu	Vuu
வ	வா	வி	வீ	வு	வூ
وَ	وَا	وِ	وِيْ	وُ	وُوْ

வெ	வே	வை	வொ	வோ	வௌ
وِ	وِيْ	وَيْ	وٗ	وَٗ	وَوْ
Ve	Vee	Vai	Vo	Voo	vau
வெ	வே	வை	வொ	வோ	வௌ
وِ	وِيْ	وَيْ	وٗ	وَٗ	وَوْ
Ve	Vee	Vai	Vo	Voo	vau

ழ	ழா	ழி	ழீ	ழு	ழூ
ضَ	ضَا	ضِ	ضِيْ	ضُ	ضُوْ
Zha	Zhaa	Zhi	Zhii	Zhu	Zhuu

ழெ	ழே	ழை	ழொ	ழோ	ழௌ
ضِ	ضِيْ	ضَيْ	ضَ	ضَوْ	ضَوْ
Zhe	Zhee	Zhai	Zho	Zhoo	zhau

ள	ளா	ளி	ளீ	ளு	ளூ
صَ	صَا	صِ	صِيْ	صُ	صُوْ
La	Laa	Li	Lii	Lu	Luu

ளெ	ளே	ளை	ளொ	ளோ	ளௌ
صِ	صِيْ	صَيْ	صَ	صَوْ	صَوْ
Le	Lee	Lai	Lo	Loo	Lau

ற	றா	றி	றீ	று	றூ
رَ	رَا	رِ	رِي	رُ	رُو
Ra	Raa	Ri	Rii	Ru	Ruu
رَ	رَا	رِ	رِي	رُ	رُو

றெ	றே	றை	றொ	றோ	றௌ
رِ	رِيْ	رَيْ	رُ	رُوْ	رَوْ
Re	Ree	Rai	Ro	Roo	Rau
	رِيْ	رَيْ	رُ	رُوْ	رَوْ

ன	னா	னி	னீ	னு	னூ
نَ	نَا	نِ	نِيْ	نُ	نُوْ
Na	Naa	Ni	Nii	Nu	Nuu
نَ	نَا	نِ	نِيْ	نُ	نُوْ

னெ	னே	னை	னொ	னோ	னௌ
نِ	نِيْ	نَيْ	نٗ	نٗوْ	نَوْ
Ne	Nee	Nai	No	Noo	Nau
نِ	نِيْ	نَيْ	نٗ	نَوْ	نَوْ

ಜ	ಜಾ	ಜಿ	ಜೀ	ಜು	ಜೂ
جَ	جَا	جِ	جِيْ	جُ	جُوْ
ja	jaa	ji	jii	ju	juu

ஜெ	ஜே	ஜை	ஜொ	ஜோ	ஜௌ
جَ	جِيْ	جَيْ	جُ	جُوْ	جَوْ
je	jee	jai	jo	joo	jau
ஜெ	ஜே	ஜை	ஜொ	ஜோ	ஜௌ
جَ	جِيْ	جَيْ	جُ	جُوْ	جَوْ
je	jee	jai	jo	joo	jau

ஷ	ஷா	ஷி	ஷீ	ஷு	ஷூ
شَ	شَا	شِ	شِيْ	شُ	شُوْ
Sha	Shaa	Shi	Shii	Shu	Shuu
شَ	شَا	شِ	شِيْ	شُ	شُوْ

ஷெ	ஷே	ஷை	ஷொ	ஷோ	ஷௌ
شِ	شِيْ	شَيْ	شَئ	شُوْ	شَوْ
She	Shee	Shai	Sho	Shoo	Shau
ஷெ	ஷே	ஷை	ஷொ	ஷோ	ஷௌ
شِ	شِيْ	شَيْ	شَئ	شُوْ	شَوْ

സ	സാ	സി	സീ	സു	സൂ
سَ	سَا	سِ	سِيْ	سُ	سُوْ
sa	saa	si	sii	su	suu

സെ	സേ	സൈ	സൊ	സോ	സൌ
سِ	سِيْ	سَيْ	سًٔ	سًوْ	سَوْ
se	see	sai	so	soo	sau
سِ	سِيْ	سَيْ	سًٔ	سًوْ	سَوْ

ஹ	ஹா	ஹி	ஹீ	ஹு	ஹூ
حَ	حَا	حِ	حِيْ	حُ	حُوْ
ha	haa	hi	hii	hu	huu

ஹெ	ஹே	ஹை	ஹொ	ஹோ	ஹௌ
حِ	حِيْ	حَيْ	حُ	حُوْ	حَوْ
he	hee	hai	ho	hoo	hau
ஹெ	ஹே	ஹை	ஹொ	ஹோ	ஹௌ

சூழி	சூழா	சூழி	சூழீ	சூழு	சூழூ
دْچ	دْجَا	دْجِ	دْجِيْ	دْجُ	دْجُوْ
kṣa	kṣaa	kṣi	kṣii	kṣu	kṣuu
دْچ	دْجَا	دْجِ	دْجِيْ	دْجُ	دْجُوْ
kṣa	kṣaa	kṣi	kṣii	kṣu	kṣuu

செஷ	சேஷ	சைஷ	செஷா	சேஷா	செஷௌ
بْچِ	پْچِي	بْچَيْ	بُّچ	بُّچْو	بْچَوْ
kṣe	kṣee	kṣai	kṣho	kṣhoo	kṣau

K	Ng	S	Nj	T	N
க்	ங்	ச்	ஞ்	ட்	ண்
كْ	عْ	چْ	نْ	دْ	نْ

Th	n	P	M	Y	R
த்	ந்	ப	ம்	ன	ற
ث	ن	ڣ	مْ	ي	ژ

L	V	Zh	L	R	N
ல்	வ்	ழ்	ள்	ற்	ன்
ﻝْ	وْ	ضْ	صْ	رْ	نْ

J	Sh	S	H	kṣ	
ஜ	ஷ	ஸ	ஹ	க்ஷ	
جْ	شْ	سْ	خْ	چْدْ	

12.0 Conclusion

The important reason for the unfamiliarity of Arwi is the lack of competitive printing facilities. Printing of Arwi books is a very complicated and tedious process. The early 20th century adoption of Urdu as the dominant Islamic school curriculum, ethnocentrically unconcerned with Arwi which has a different, southern South Asia based cultural and historical genesis is also an another reason for its decline. This literature has not received much attention in the later part of the 20th century.

The issues and challenges in encoding Arwi can be solved by adopting Unicode characters to type Arwi language .Today the printing system needs such encoding solutions, in order to make the task of printing and publishing the Arwi books as easier ones. There are only few hundreds of Arwi books were published, so far in different parts of Asia, and more than 4000 books were unpublished and these books were available in handwritten or in manuscript form. To publish these literary works, we are badly in need of printing and encoding solutions. If they got published, then these works may be introduced as OSS (open source software) products to all readers of the world such as Wikipedia and others.

References

1. Maharoof, M M M. Spoken Tamil dialect of the Muslims of Sri Lanka: Language as Identity classifier. Karach: IRI, 1995. Print.

2. Rahim, M R M Abdul.: Islamia Kalai Kalanjiam. Madras: Universal Publishers, 1976. Print.

3. Rahman, H Abdul. Origin and Development of Arabu-Tamil in Tamil Nadu. Madras: University of Madras, 1985. M Phil Diss..

4. Samuel, G John. Tamil as a classical Language. Chennai:Institute of Asian Studies, 2010. Print.

5. Shuaib, Tayka. Arabic, Arwi and Persian in Sarandib and Tamil Nadu. Chennai:Aroosia Trust, 1993. Print.

6. Zubair, K M A Ahamed. al-Lisan al-Arwi.New Delhi: ICCR, 2006. Print.

7. Zubair, K M A Ahamed. Arwi or Arabu-Tamil. Saarbrucken: Lambert Academic Publishing, 2014. Print.

Online available sources

8. http://www.unicode.org/versions/Unicode6.0.0/

9. http://en.wikipedia.org/wiki/Arabic_%28Unicode_block%29

10. http://en.wikipedia.org/wiki/Arabic_Presentation_Forms-A

11. http://en.wikipedia.org/wiki/Arabic_Presentation_Forms-B

12. http://en.wikipedia.org/wiki/Arabic_Mathematical_Alphabetic_Symbols

13. http://en.wikipedia.org/wiki/Arabic-Indic_digits#Symbols

14. http://www.unicode.org/charts/PDF/U0600.pdf

15. http://en.wikipedia.org/wiki/Arwi

Buy your books fast and straightforward online - at one of world's fastest growing online book stores! Environmentally sound due to Print-on-Demand technologies.

Buy your books online at
www.morebooks.shop

Kaufen Sie Ihre Bücher schnell und unkompliziert online – auf einer der am schnellsten wachsenden Buchhandelsplattformen weltweit! Dank Print-On-Demand umwelt- und ressourcenschonend produzi ert.

Bücher schneller online kaufen
www.morebooks.shop

Printed by Books on Demand GmbH, Norderstedt / Germany